Catalina Bapt~~ist~~

God Made the Sea, the Sand, and Me

ELIZABETH ELAINE WATSON
Illustrated by H. Don Fields

For Brian and Bruce

BROADMAN PRESS
Nashville, Tennessee

© Copyright 1978 ● Broadman Press.
All rights reserved.
4242-54
ISBN: 0-8054-4254-5

Dewey Decimal Classification: C240
Subject heading: GOD
Printed in the United States of America

God made all things. He made the sea. He made the sand. And God made me.

God made a smile for me to wear when I am happy.

... when I stand on the beach and let the waves cover my feet.

... when I build a castle in the sand.

. . . when I eat ice cream on a picnic.
God made the sea. He made the sand. And God made me.

God made some teardrops that roll down my cheek when I am sad.

. . . when I fall and cut my knee.

. . . when the waves wash away my sand castle.

. . . when the water splashes in my face.

God made the sea. He made the sand. And God made me.

God gave me two eyes to see his beautiful world.

. . . to see the sea gulls flying over the water.

. . . to see the fish swimming under the water.

. . . to see the sunshine that warms the earth and makes the water sparkle.

God made the sea. He made the sand. And God made me.

God gave me two feet to run and jump and play.

. . . to take walks along the sandy beach and hunt for seashells.

. . . to jump and run when the waves chase me and wash away my footprints.

God made the sea. He made the sand. And God made me.

God made my mother for me to love. She tucks me into bed at night. She makes my hurt knee feel better.

God made my daddy for me to love. He lifts me up over the waves when we swim together. He has a big strong hand that's nice to hold when I am afraid.

God made the nighttime for me to rest and sleep. The sea and the sand wait for me to come back in the morning and play some more.

God made a book for me to read. It's called the Bible. The Bible tells me all about God. It tells me that God made all things. It tells me that God loved me even before he made the sea, the sand, and me. God loved me first. I want to love him best.

Thank you, God, for making the sea, the sand, and me.